CREATIVE HOUSEHOLD TIPS
FOR
SURVIVING A RECESSION

Natalie A. Conway

Copyright © 2009

All rights reserved – Natalie A. Conway

No part of this book may be reproduced or transmitted in any form or by any means, graphic, electronic, or mechanical, including photocopying, recording, taping, or by any information storage retrieval system, without the permission, in writing, from the publisher.

ISBN: 1450577628   EAN-13 9781450577625

Table of Contents

Introduction 11

1. The State of Your Economy 15

2. Defining Recession 19

3. Saving Money at Home 23

4. Supermarket Savings 33

5. Walking into Savings 43

6. Home-Cooked Take-Out 55

7. A Change of Habit 63

8. Bringing Hope Home 71

Dedication

This book is dedicated
to my mom,
Lilian, my best friend.

Acknowledgements

Special thanks to my hardworking editor and writer, Sandy Tritt, and her very talented staff at Inspiration for Writers, Inc. (www.InspirationForWriters.com).

"They say that time changes things, but you actually have to change them yourself."

-Andy Warhol

Introduction

"**M**ommy, are we going to lose our house?" is the most frequently asked question in our home.

Increasing numbers of people face homelessness. Even children fear losing their homes. Tough economic times leave many of us with reduced incomes; we face uncertainty about the future while worrying about our quality of life. We even worry if we can afford day-to-day necessities.

Using creative ideas to save money and reduce expenses is one of the ways our household makes up for what we lack in income.

I hope the ideas you find in this book will help you make it through the recession.

Where to Begin

Looking in the mirror is a good place to start. See yourself as a resource.

Evaluate all areas of your household budget, paying special attention to expenses you can reduce or possibly eliminate. Review the ideas in this book to help you.

Make timely decisions. For many of us, simply making a decision is an important first step. Set a deadline, and realize that no decision means no change will occur.

Ways to Save Money and Energy

- Use the most energy efficient type of light bulb for your lighting needs.

- Window coverings can help keep your home warmer in winter and cooler in summer when used to shut out the sun during hot days and close out drafts during cooler months.

- Quick fixes such as caulking and weather stripping around doors and windows help seal your home from cold drafts. In cooler months, this can help retain the heat in your home if you lose power for an extended period of time.

- Landscaping your yard can help lower air conditioning costs. Planting trees and shrubs can provide shade to your home in the summer, which helps your home stay cooler and lessens the work of your air conditioner.

"Carefully positioned trees can save up to 25% of the energy a typical household uses for energy. Research shows that daytime air temperatures can be 3 to 6 degrees cooler in tree-shaded neighborhoods than in treeless ones."[1]

1

The State of Your Economy

For many people, shortened workweeks or layoffs brought on by the recession adds to existing financial problems, widening the gap between income and expenses.

In a more reliable economy, making a career change to earn more money or finding a better paying job can decrease or eventually eliminate this gap.

However, during a recession, jobs can be harder to find. So, if your income does not currently meet your expenses, it's time to start thinking creatively about cutting costs. Look around your home and make a plan to reduce whatever expenses you can.

For many of us, getting through a recession means changing how we spend money. These changes can leave us with improved spending and saving habits long after the recession has come and gone.

Some Ways to Save Money

- Transfer credit card balances to new accounts that offer free or lower finance charges—but be sure to read the fine print to see if there's a one-time transfer charge. You can also contact your current credit card carrier and ask for a reduction in rates.

- Add water to dilute drinks. Not only does this create more servings, but it helps your family drink more of one of the healthiest beverages—water!

- Add bread crumbs to ground beef to make it go further. Add a little Worcestershire sauce to increase moisture and give more flavor.

- Fill up on food samples at the grocery store.

- Return items that haven't been opened to the store for a cash refund. Even if you don't have the receipt, you can usually get store credit and use the money for something else you need.

Visit www.recessionrelieftips.com for more money-saving tips and ideas to help your household.

Making Changes to Get By

In response to widespread unemployment, many households are making necessary lifestyle changes and other sacrifices to simply "get through the day."

Reaching the end of a day with adequate food, shelter and warmth becomes a considerable achievement instead of an expectation.

Adjusting to a reduced income begins with spending less money for things we *want*—as well as finding ways to spend less for things we *need*.

Instead of going out for dinner, enjoy a backyard barbeque. Instead of driving somewhere for an outing or a day trip, take a leisurely walk or cycle to a nearby park.

Both small and large changes give our finances some relief as we find ways to survive the recession.

2

Defining Recession

The World Book Encyclopedia defines *recession* as "a decline in overall business activity. During a nationwide recession, a country suffers a drop in buying, selling, and production and a rise in unemployment."[2]

Unemployment and underemployment create financial problems. But there are things you can do before the pink slip arrives to help lessen the stress of a drop in income.

For example, instead of paying the minimum amount due on utility bills, pay a little more. This will give some breathing room when income drops, allowing for smaller payments or even allowing for a skipped payment.

Be aware that some bills, such as credit card payments, home loans, car loans, and so forth, may still require the minimum monthly payment each month regardless of overpayments in previous months.

Finding ways to reduce spending each day makes a difference in how effectively we balance our budget at the end of the month.

Getting Through the Difficult Days
During a recession, every day can be a difficult day. My days begin and end with finding ways to minimize our spending.

On hot summer days when my children cool off by running through sprinklers, I give them a bottle of shampoo and a bar of soap. Also, moving the sprinklers frequently allows the lawn to get watered at the same time. This method of taking showers becomes a "fun-filled" money-saving event.

Instead of going out for dinner and a movie, we borrow a DVD from the library for free, then make our own pizza (ready-to-bake pizza crusts, sauce, shredded cheese and a few toppings).

Instead of going somewhere and paying to be entertained, we rediscover the joy of board games. Not only are they fun, but the family grows closer as they play together instead of "being entertained."

Finding ways to survive the recession can make happy memories.

Help children understand the recession's effect on day-to-day life by:

- Keeping them informed.
- Encouraging them to be hopeful by example.
- Involving them in decisions to save money, especially when giving up something enjoyable.

And remember: opportunity is where you find it. If you've lost your job or if your hours have been reduced, use this as an opportunity to do something you've wanted to do but haven't had time, such as going back to school, learning a new craft or hobby, volunteering, or whatever your heart desires.

3

Saving Money at Home

Having a limited social life is a real money saver. Spending more time at home gives me the opportunity to find more ways to save money.

Using Water to Save Water

Water can be reused in multiple ways. Almost every day my family leaves unfinished glasses or bottles of water around the house. Instead of pouring unused water down the drain, I use it to rinse recyclable bottles, cans, and other containers, or for other household uses, such as watering houseplants.

I then run remaining water through the garbage disposal to help rinse away any residue. This saves money while conserving one of our natural resources.

Your local home improvement store is a good source of help and information for things you can do to decrease your water consumption with little investment.

Also, bills from the utility company will often include informative inserts, promotions or coupons for free or discounted products.

The End of a Good Thing
Using all the slices in a loaf of bread is another way to save money.

Throwing away the crusts with the wrapper is the same as throwing away money.

I usually buy four loaves of bread a week. Using every slice, including the crusty ends, saves more than twenty loaves of bread a year. If your family doesn't like the taste of the crusts, use them as hamburger buns or toss them into a freezer bag to make croutons or to mix in with ground beef.

Money-Saving Socks
Finding a pair of matching socks around our house sometimes becomes an adventure no one wants to participate in.

If possible, buy the same brand and a single color of socks so you'll have any number of matches available. But if that isn't possible or if you're already stuck with misfits, get creative.

Match up possible pairs, or make combinations that complement colors in outfits—like a pink sock on one foot and a yellow on the other to go with a pink and yellow skirt.

Creating a Restful Routine

Our lives are filled with money-saving ideas waiting to be discovered. Some of the best ways to save *time* can also be great ways to save *money*. One of my single friends developed the following routine to reduce the time she spends doing laundry:

She sleeps on one side of her bed several days in a row, then sleeps on the other side for several more days. Thus, she can go twice as long before doing laundry. Placing a barrier the length of the bed keeps her from rolling onto the other side while she sleeps.

This time-saving routine cuts costs for water, power and laundry detergent, while lessening how often she does one of her most tiresome chores.

Her routine shows us how creative thinking can reduce expenses incurred while doing household chores.

Examples of Money-Saving Routines Around the Home

- "Turn off computers and monitors. Unplug electronics with a stand-by mode, chargers for cordless phones, etc., when not being used."[3]

- Reorganize your routine so you do the bulk of your reading during the day. Also, encourage children to develop the habit of doing homework *earlier* rather than *later* in the day to use minimal or no lighting, thus reducing electricity use.

- When cooking, using a lid to cover a pot or pan lets you use a lower temperature on your stove.[4]

- Clean your dryer lint filter before putting in a new load of clothes to help your dryer work more efficiently, thus saving energy costs.[5]

- Using an outdoor clothesline or an indoor drying rack is a "back to basics" way to give yourself a break on your power bill.

- Disposable cups—or, better yet, a reusable cup—in the bathroom can help younger children use less water while brushing their teeth.

Notes: Ways I Can Save Money at Home

Example: I can save money by using all the slices in a loaf of bread, including the crusts.

_____
_____
_____
_____
_____
_____
_____
_____
_____
_____
_____
_____
_____
_____
_____
_____

Working it Out: Money-Saving Calculations for Home

Example: When I use all slices in a loaf of bread, including crusty ends, I use twenty fewer loaves of bread a year.

20 loaves x $2.50 per loaf = $50.00 savings

_____
_____
_____
_____
_____
_____
_____
_____
_____
_____
_____
_____
_____

4

Supermarket Savings

The recession makes my weekly trip to the grocery store one of my easiest errands. I no longer have to push around a heavy shopping cart—unless one of my kids wants a ride. If possible, though, try to leave children at home when you shop. That way, you can avoid the "Mommy, can I" routine.

Having less money to buy groceries means I spend less time shopping—which leaves more time to spend with friends and family. This is one of the most enjoyable changes the recession has added to my life.

Clip Coupons

If you are not already clipping coupons, now is a great time to start. Newspapers, websites and grocery store advertisements are the most common sources.

Some stores will double or even triple coupons on certain days, and some stores will offer sales that will complement the coupons in the Sunday paper. Plan your shopping to make the most of your coupons.

Savings Tip: Set aside the money you save using coupons for something special—even if that something is to top-off your gas tank once a month.

Produce in Season

When you buy fruits and vegetables in season, they are generally of better quality and cost less. If you are unsure which fruits or vegetables are in season, ask the produce clerk or store manager.

"On Sale" Items

"On sale" is not always the best buy. I compare the price per unit for all items, especially when they're "on sale." Sometimes a different brand or items with a bonus amount of product are comparable to sale items.

Menu Shop
Create a menu for the entire week, then plan your shopping list around your menu. Schedule one day for leftovers to give yourself a night off from making dinner—or for days when afterschool activities leave little time for meal preparation.

Grocery List
Making a grocery list works to save money when I stick to buying only items I have on my list. It also helps me to remember all the things I need, saving me the inconvenience of an extra trip to the store for something I might have missed if I hadn't made a list.

Look-a-likes
Some varieties of fruits and vegetables look alike. A visible sticker on at least one item lessens the chance of a pricing error and helps the cashier identify the produce.

Example: At a glance, a "hothouse tomato" and a "tomato on the vine" look similar, but one variety is more expensive than the other.

Home Cooking
One of the things I enjoy most is preparing meals for my family. Home cooking is generally less expensive and more nutritious than eating prepared or packaged meals.

Farmers' Markets
Locally grown produce can be less expensive and fresher—plus it gives us the opportunity to support local farmers.

Eat Before Shopping
Being hungry when shopping for groceries can make items we don't normally eat look appetizing. As a result, we can spend money for foods we may not need or that are unhealthy—and expensive.

Think Big
Individually packaged foods offer convenience in many ways except to our budgets. Buying larger packages of food and dividing them into smaller bags or containers at home can save money.

"A Green Garden" for a Greener Wallet
Growing a small garden can save money on your grocery bill. A minimal investment in seed packets, fertilizer, water, etc., can create a bounty of fresh produce.

Besides eating produce fresh from the garden, you can freeze or can it to enjoy all year long.

Bonus: Not only are fresh vegetables healthy to eat, but the exercise and fresh air received in tending a garden is an added benefit.

"Goof-Proof" Supermarket Checklist

- Weigh everything not packaged: fruits, vegetables, bulk items, etc. Estimating the costs of these items ahead of time helps to stay on budget.

- When buying produce, look for a sticker on at least one item of every type purchased.

- Follow-up at the check stand to ensure the price per pound entered by the cashier and the assigned sticker price are the same.

- When buying multiples of the same item, keep track of how many you purchased and compare your total to the number of items scanned by the cashier. Correcting mistakes at the check stand saves time, money and gas for a return trip.

- Make sure all items scanned at the checkout are bagged and placed in your cart.

Notes: Ways I Save Money When Buying Groceries

Examples: 1. I make a shopping list and buy only the items on my list.

2. I compare "bonus amount" products to their "on sale" counterparts to make sure I get the best deal available.

_____
_____
_____
_____
_____
_____
_____
_____
_____
_____
_____
_____

Working It Out: Money Saving Calculations at the Grocery Store

Example: A box of cereal with a **25% bonus** selling at regular price can be a good buy.
25% x 4 boxes = one **free** box after buying the fourth box. Check with the store manager for an estimate of how long a promotion will run. This helps you plan your spending if you can't afford to stock up in one trip.

_____
_____
_____
_____
_____
_____
_____
_____
_____

5

Walking Into Savings

I listened to a couple reminisce about driving long distances to lull their kids to sleep. Unfortunately, this parenting trick is no longer practical because we can't afford the expense of extra gas.

Instead, today's families must find ways to save money by driving less.

Using the car less by walking, cycling and planning errands ahead of time helps to reduce gas expense and lessens emissions released into our environment.

Everyday Ways to Save Gas

1. Stay home one or more days a week.

2. Organize carpools with friends, neighbors and family.

3. Make an effort to plan more than one stop when out.

"Several short trips taken from a cold start can use twice as much fuel as one trip covering the same distance when the engine is warm."[6]

4. When possible, park a short distance away from where you're going and walk instead of driving, depending on the weather and time limitations.

5. If at all possible, plan your route to make use of side streets to avoid traffic lights that have a long wait.

6. When going to the mall, don't search for a *good* parking space. Instead, take the first adequate one.

7. When there is a long line for drive-through service, park your car and go inside.

8. Keep to the manufacturer's recommended maintenance schedule for your car. Look for coupons, discount offers and promotions for these services in the mail, online and in newspapers.

- "Keeping your tires properly inflated and aligned can increase mileage by up to 3%."[7]

- "An extra 100 pounds in the trunk can reduce fuel economy by up to 2%."[8]

Resources to Save Gas and Energy
The Federal Trade Commission's online website, http://www.ftc.gov/bcp/edu/microsites/energysavings/flash.html, has a wide range of articles that you can download or print.

"Saving Money at the Gas Pump: A Bumper-to-Bumper Guide," features money-saving tips, advice and ideas for car maintenance, performance and fuel economy.

Using the Owner's Manual
Improved fuel economy begins with following the recommendations in your owner's manual for oil changes, the grade of motor oil and the octane level of gas best suited for your car.

"Keeping your engine tuned according to your owner's manual can increase gas mileage by an average of 4% depending on the condition of the car."[9]

Ways to Improve Fuel Economy

1. Pack your car and organize your purse ahead of time with what you need for errands or the day's activities. This lessens the chance that you will remember something you need after you start your car, or worse, after you've already driven part way.

2. Start your car *after* rather than *before* you buckle your seatbelt.

"Idling gets you 0 miles per gallon. The best way to warm up a vehicle is to drive it. No more than 30 seconds on a winter day is needed."[10]

3. Plan a few extra minutes to get to appointments and other commitments. Being in a hurry can distract from driving habits that benefit fuel economy.

"You can improve in-town gas mileage by up to 5% by driving gently."[11]

4. When traveling somewhere for the first time, use a resource for reliable directions. If your car is not equipped with a navigation system, use the internet, a map, or write down directions given verbally.

Uncertainty about the route, location or address of your destination can increase your fuel consumption—"wrong turns" waste both time and gas.

5. Keep in mind that driving within posted limits contributes to your safety and fuel efficiency.

"Gas mileage decreases rapidly at speeds above sixty miles per hour."[12]

Get Help Using Your Thermostat

"The average household spends more than $2,200 a year on energy bills—nearly half of which goes to heating and cooling. Homeowners can save about $180 a year by properly setting their programmable thermostats and maintaining those settings."[13]

Programmable thermostats have energy saving features that include multiple temperature settings for each day of the week.

"Depending on your family's schedule, you can see significant savings by sticking to those settings or adjusting them as appropriate for your family. The key is to establish a program that automatically reduces heating and cooling in your home when you don't need as much."[14]

If your home is not equipped with a programmable thermostat, manual thermostats can also be adjusted daily and used effectively to reduce heating and cooling costs.

Download a free copy of "Saving Starts @ Home: The Inside Story on Conserving Energy," which provides many helpful hints on saving money and creating a more energy-efficient home. Just go to
http://www.ftc.gov/energysavings.

Notes: Things I Can Do to Save Car Expenses and Energy

Examples: walking, cycling and carpooling helps me lower my gas expense

_____
_____
_____
_____
_____
_____
_____
_____
_____
_____
_____
_____
_____
_____
_____

Working It Out: Money Saving Calculations to Use Less Energy

Examples:
- I walked and cycled about 700 miles this year instead of driving;
- my car gets about 20 miles per gallon;
- I saved approximately 35 gallons of gas;
- average price of gas this year has been $3.25 per gallon

$3.25
X 35 gallons
Savings = $113.75

_____
_____
_____
_____
_____
_____

6

Home-Cooked Take-Out

It's been my experience that the real joy of cooking happens when someone else does it. Since going out for dinner is expensive, it's reserved for special occasions.

Occasionally, including take-out or prepared foods as part of a home-cooked meal allows my family to enjoy some of our favorite restaurant dinners at a reasonable price. Following are examples of affordable meals I create for my family.

Also, if your family hates leftovers, get creative. Instead of having "leftovers," have Salad Bar Night. Cut leftover meats into cubes, leave leftover veggies cold (unless someone really wants them hot), and give everything a stir so it looks appetizing.

Put up a side table to hold all the choices, add a fresh bowl of lettuce and another new item, such as applesauce, mandarin oranges, cottage cheese, or cheese, and you have an "all you can eat buffet." You'll find that soon "Salad Bar Night" is everyone's favorite meal.

DINNER 1

> Rotisserie Chicken
> Potatoes/Rice
> Vegetable

A rotisserie chicken from the grocery store is an easy meal starter. It's reasonably priced and makes a nutritious dinner.

Adding rice or potatoes and a vegetable makes it a winning recipe for affordability. Any leftover chicken is great for making soup, sandwiches or a casserole.

DINNER 2

> Dollar/Value Menu Cheeseburgers
> Fries or Onion Rings from your freezer
> Bottle or can of your favorite soft drink

Cheeseburgers, fries or onion rings, and a soft drink is the dinner of choice in our home. Restaurants tend to attract us by offering the "main dish"—the burgers—at a great price. But the price of fries and soft drinks makes the dinner much more expensive.

So, pick up burgers from a restaurant with a dollar/value menu, then toss some frozen fries or onion rings in the oven. Soft drinks are always much less expensive when bought in cases and served from home.

Any leftover soda can be used for making ice cream floats for an after-dinner treat.

DINNER 3

> A Single Entrée (from a Chinese Restaurant)
> Chicken Nuggets with sweet and sour sauce
> Rice or Noodles (made at home)

Chinese Cuisine gets a five star rating at our house. Making sweet & sour chicken, a side dish of rice or noodles, and buying one entrée from a Chinese restaurant is my shortcut to affordability for this dinner.

Leftover rice or noodles can be combined with chicken from **DINNER 1** in soup or a casserole.

Notes: Shortcuts: Home-Cooked Take-Out

Examples:
- rotisserie chicken
- steamed rice
- 1 can green beans

Working It Out: Shortcuts: Home-Cooked Take-Out

Example: Rotisserie Chicken Dinner (approx. 4-6 servings)

Items to add to shopping list:
rotisserie chicken, vegetable and rice.

*This dinner is quick, easy, and usually costs less than $10.00 to prepare.

_____
_____
_____
_____
_____
_____
_____
_____
_____
_____

7

A Change of Habit

"Why did you pay the power bill when you haven't gotten a shut-off notice?" one of my neighbors asked me after I received an insufficient funds notice from the bank.

My neighbor didn't want me to put my family at risk. She was trying to help me save money.

When there are no other consequences to consider, paying bills in order of late fees, highest to lowest, can save money. This helps us organize expenses when we don't have enough money to pay all our bills on time.

Ways to Budget Late Fees:
1. Keep track of grace periods for all accounts. A grace period allows *extra time* to pay without a late fee or penalty.

2. Reorganize your payment schedule by the amount of associated late fees and penalties.

3. Make phone calls to arrange payment options before a bill is considered late.

4. When using a credit card, pay as much as possible before the due date to reduce finance charges.

A Shoestring Budget

One of my sons had holes in his running shoes. Rainy weather loosened the duct tape holding them together.

At the end of the school day, his shoes and socks were wet. Since, at this time, we could only afford one pair of shoes per child, I knew I had to get creative.

Keeping him home until we had money to buy his shoes was not a practical solution. So, I made arrangements to pay one of our bills late.

The late fee was less than the cost of cold medicine, which he would've needed if he continued to come home with wet shoes and socks.

Taking care of my family's needs by paying bills late is not typically what I do to get through a normal day, but during a recession, many of us have to deal with circumstances that are anything but normal.

A Book for a Child
My daughter needed a check to buy a book at school. After paying for major car repairs, we had very little money on hand.

Using a credit card for an expense I normally pay with cash left enough money in the bank to cover the cost of the book.

Sending a payment to the credit card company before the grace period ended and ordering her book just before the deadline made this special purchase possible while avoiding finance charges.

Notes:

Ways to Minimize Late Fees:

Example:

These bills have the same due date, but different late fees.

Water bill: $70   late fee = $10.00
Power bill: $150 late fee = 1% ($1.50)
Car payment: $375 late fee = $37.50

-paying the car payment first will save money in fees

_____
_____
_____
_____
_____
_____
_____
_____
_____

Working it Out: Money Saving Calculations for Late Fees

Budget for late fees this month-
-water bill, late fee: $10.00 -pay second
-power bill, late fee: $ 1.50 -pay last
-car payment, late fee: $37.50 -pay first

8

Bringing Hope Home

While getting through the recession brings little satisfaction and keeping up with expenses can become overwhelming, a written list of goals helps me stay motivated and hopeful.

My Goals:
- To have enough money to buy groceries without having to put things back at the check stand.

- To enjoy a walk for its health benefits instead of its money-saving benefits.

- To have a month of no overdue bills and late fees.

- To have the choice of buying new or used clothing.

- To be able to put gas in the car to enjoy a day trip with my family.

- To take a vacation.

Be a Survival Statistic

To help our families get through the recession, we sometimes must give up things we enjoy. Family vacations have been shortened to day trips, and outings for treats like ice cream happen less often.

Even though we are forced to cope with less, there are gains to be realized in other aspects of our lives.

Being more thoughtful about using money is a "skill" many of us will benefit from.

Enjoying time with our friends and families without spending money is a healing process that costs nothing.

On a sunny midsummer afternoon while relaxing, I watched my kids play quietly on our front porch, and I realized the things I do matter.

Making an effort to survive the recession is an accomplishment of greater value than many material things we can provide.

Things to Think About

Be hopeful. Dealing with ups and downs is simply part of life.

Do something every day to either save money or make money last longer.

Think more creatively. Start with the ideas in this book and then add your own.

Have simple goals that bring you personal satisfaction. You don't need a Disney vacation to have fun—nor do you need the latest model car. Joy can be found by spending time with those you love.

Know that saving pennies adds up to dollars that can one day make a difference.

It is not the strongest of the species that survives, nor the most intelligent, but the one most responsive to change.

-Charles Darwin

BIBLIOGRAPHY

Fowles, Debbie. *The Everything Personal Finance In Your 20'S & 30's Book*. Adams Media, an F+W Publications Company. 2004.

Gieke, Ernestine. *Dollars and Sense. Managing Your Money*. Reed & Professional Publishing. Published by Heinemann Library. 2003.

Morris, Claire E., "Recession," in *World Book Encyclopedia*. World Book Inc. 2009.

Tyson Eric, Shell Jim. *Small Business for Dummies. 3rd Edition*. Wiley Publishing, Inc. 2008.

Woman's Day. *Living Fiscally Fit. 1,000 Ways to Get out of Debt & Build Financial Wealth*. Filipacchi Publishing USA, Inc. 2008.

Online Bibliography

Federal Trade Commission. "Good, Better, Best: How to Improve Gas Mileage." Available at http://www.ftc.gov/bcp/edu/pubs/consumer/alerts/alt064.shtm; Internet.

Federal Trade Commission, "Saving Money at the Gas Pump: A Bumper-to-Bumper Guide." Available at http://www.ftc.gov/bcp/edu/microsites/energysavings/savegas/flash.html; Internet.

Federal Trade Commission, "Saving Starts @ Home: The Inside Story on Conserving Energy," available at http://www.ftc.gov/energysavings; Internet.

US Department of Energy, "Energy Savers-Tips on Saving Money and Energy at Home," available at http://www1.eere.energy.gov/consumer/tips; Internet.

US Environmental Protection Agency, US Department of Energy - Energy Star, available at http://www.energystar.gov/index.cfm?c=thermostats.pr_thermostats; Internet.

End Notes

[1] US Department of Energy, "Energy Savers, Tips on Saving Money at Home," available from http://www1.eere.energy.gov/consumer/tips/landscaping.html; Internet. Accessed 22 January 2009.

[2] Clair E. Morris, "Recession," in *World Book Encyclopedia*, 2009 ed., volume Q-R p.162

[3] U.S. Department of Energy, "Energy Savers, Tips on Saving Money at Home," available from http://www1.eere.energy.gov/consumer/tips/save_energy.html; Internet. Accessed 22 January 2009.

[4] Federal Trade Commission, "Saving Starts @ Home: The Inside Story on Conserving Energy," available from http://www.ftc.gov/bcp/edu/microsites/energysavings/kitchen.htm; Internet. Accessed 24 April 2009.

[5] Ibid.

[6] Federal Trade Commission, "Saving Money at the Gas Pump: A Bumper-to-Bumper Guide," available from http://www.ftc.gov/bcp/edu/microsites/energysavings/savegas/flash.html; Internet. Accessed 24 April 2009.

[7] Ibid.

[8] Ibid.

[9] Federal Trade Commission, "Good, Better, Best: How to Improve Gas Mileage," available from http://www.ftc.gov/bcp/edu/pubs/consumer/alerts/alt064.shtm; Internet. Accessed 24 April 2009.

[10] US Department of Energy, "Energy Savers, Tips on Saving Money at Home," available from http://www1.eere.energy.gov/consumer/tips/driving.html; Internet. Accessed 22 January 2009.

[11] Federal Trade Commission, "Saving Money at the Gas Pump: A Bumper-to-Bumper Guide," available from

http://www.ftc.gov/bcp/edu/microsites/energysavings/savegas/flash.html; Internet. Accessed 24 April 2009.

[12] Ibid.

[13] US Environmental Protection Agency ,US Department of Energy - Energy Star. "Typical House Factoid Memo," Lawrence Berkeley National Laboratory; available from http://www.energystar.gov/index.cfm?c=thermostats.pr_thermostats; Internet. Accessed 22 January 2009.

[14] Ibid.

Made in the USA
Charleston, SC
13 March 2010